Reading Hieroglyphs

Ancient Egyptian Stela

Reading & Answer Book

ISBN-13: 978-1517010379

ISBN-10: 1517010373

http://arkpublishing.co.uk

Bernard Paul Badham

'Horus-Akhety (Horus of the Two Horizons), the Behdetite (Edfu), Great God'

Ancient Egyptian Stela

A stela (plural stelas or stelæ, from Latin) is a stone or wooden slab, generally taller than it is wide, erected as a monument, very often for funerary or commemorative purposes. Stelae may be used for government notices or as territorial markers to mark borders or delineate land ownership. They very often have texts and may have decoration. This ornamentation may be inscribed, carved in relief (bas, high, etc.), or painted onto the slab.

Contents

Guideline Example of Trasliteration and Transalation:

1. Identify words using a red pen (as the ancient scribes): phonograms usually start a word and determinatives end the word, as does the single, dual and plural strokes or the feminine ending **t** or the abstract sign of a papyrus scroll.

2. Write out the phonetic transliteration (how it sounds in ancient Egyptian minus the vowels).

Golden Rule: transliterate in groups of a maximum of three words, the word groups oftern start with a preposition such as: **r, n, m** 'to, for, in' etc and end with a suffix pronoun, such as: **.f** '.he'

This is done for you in light grey, but still confirm.

3. Using a hieroglyphic dictionary* write out the literal translation of each word with alternative meanings - maintain the same word order.

4. Put into English word order - this step may be ommitted depending on the difficulty of the text.

5. Write out the full English translation:

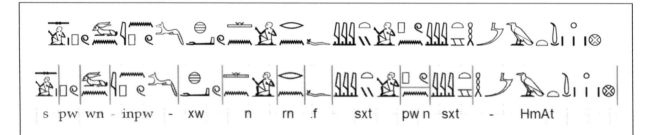

s pw wn - inpw - xw   n   rn .f   sxt   pw n sxt   -   HmAt

s pw, wn-inpw-xw.n, rn.f, sxty pw, n sxt-HmAt

man this, Wen-Inpu-Khu-en, name.his, peasant this, of Sekhet-Hemat (Wadi Natron)
this man Wen-Inpu-Khu-en this peasant of Wadi-Natron

'This man's name is Khu-en-wen-Inpu, he was a peasant of Wadi Natron.'

* *Sign List & Vocabulary Extended Edition - Learning to Read Hieroglyphs and Ancient Egyptian Art* by Bernard Paul Badham   ISBN-10: 1508549990   ISBN-13: 978-1508549994 280 pages, 4000 entries.

THE TEXTS

The Stela of Imenyseneb

Louvre Museum 269 Dynasty 13

Height: 1.07 m. Width: 0.54 m.

Top Register - Right Side

wsir xnty imtyw, nb AbDw, ptH sti ra, wp-wAwt, nb TA Dsr, mHw   lower Egypt

Osiris foremost westerners, lord Abydos, Ptah successor Ra, Wep-wawet, lord land sacred, Delta

'Osiris foremost of the Westerners, lord of Abydos, Ptah, successor of Ra, Wep-wawet, lord of the Sacred Land and Lower Egypt (in the North Delta)

Top Register - Left Side

wp-wAwt, Hrw sA wsir, wp-wAwt, SmAw, smA-tAwy

Wep-wawet, Horus son Osiris, Wep-wawet, Upper-Egypt, unite-two-lands

'Wep-wawet, Horus son of Osiris, Wep-wawet, Upper Egypt (in the South, the Nile Valley), Uniter of the Two Lands'

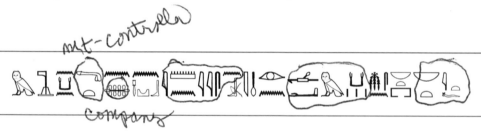

[1] nswt-Htp-di, wsir, xnty imntyw, nTr aA, nb ADw, di.f, prt-xrw, irtwt kAw Apdw, Ax wsr
king-offering-given, Osiris, foremost westerners, god great, lord Abydos, gives.he, invocation-offerings, milk cattle fowl, glorious powerful
'Offering which the King gives, Osiris, Foremost of the Westerners, the Great God, he gives invocation offerings of milk, cattle, fowl, glorious and powerful'

Wepwawet: 'Opener of the Ways,' was the jackal deity of the cult centre in Asyut, Upper Egypt. He was regarded as the 'war deity,' which led the army in battle and was also the 'opener of the ways' to and through the Duat, the Underworld, for the spirits of the deceased.'

[2] m Xrt-nTr, n kA, n mty-n-sA, n AbDw, Imny-sn, mAa-xrw, ir.n Wa-m-kAw, ms.n nbt-pr Nbt-itf
in necropolis, of ka, of controller-of-priestly-order, of Abydos, Imeny-sen, True-Voice, made-of, Wa-em-kaw, born of, mistress-house, Nebet-itef
'in the necropolis of the ka, of the controller of the priestly order of Abydos, Imeny-sen, True-of-Voice, begotten of Wa-em-kaw, born of the mistress of the house, Nebet-itef'

³ Dd.f, iwt sS, n TAti, snb, sA TAti, r iAS, n.i, m wpwt ⁴ TAti

says.he, came scribe, of vizier, Seneb, son vizier, to call/summon, for.me,

with message/mission vizier

'He says, the scribe of the vizier, Seneb, the vizier's son,

came to summon me with a mission of the vizier'

aHa.n.i, Sm.kw, Hna.f, gm.n.i, imi-r nniwt, ⁵ anxw, m xA.f

then.i, go.i, with.him, found.of.i, overseer town, Ankhu, in office.his

'The I went with him and found the overseer of the town, Ankhu, in his office'

aHa.n, rdi.n.sr, pn, wDt m Hr.i, m Dd, mk, ⁶ wDw s-wab.k, pA r-pr, n AbDw

then, put.of.official, this, command in face.my, as say, look, command make-clean.you, the utterance-house, of Abydos

**'Then this official put a command to my face, saying,
'it is commanded you purify the temple of Abydos''**

---

rid.n.k, Hmww, r nt-a.f, Hna wnwt ⁷ Hwt-nTr, nt tA spAwt, Snaw n Htp-nTr

given.to.you, craftsmen, of-the-hand.its (ritual), together-with priesthood house-god (temple), of the district/nome, labour-establishment of divine-offerings

'Craftsmen are given to you according to ritual, together with the priesthood of the temple of the nome and the labour establishment of divine offerings'

---

aHa.n, s-wab.n.i, sw, m pr-⁸Xry, pr Hry, m inbw.f, Hr-sA m Xnw

then, made-pure.of.i, it, lower-house, upper-house, in walls.it, upon outside and inside

'Then I cleaned it from the lower to the upper house through the walls outside and inside'

sS/sXaw-qdwt, Hr mH, m Drwi, m tit, m im

scribe-drawings (draughtsman), upon fill, in paint, in image, in form

'The drawing scribes were filling in paint, in the images and forms'

---

m smAwy, irt n nsw bity (xpr-kA-ra) mAa-xrw

in rejuvenate/renew, done of king-upper-lower-egypt (Kheper-ka-ra) true-voice

'in renewing what was done by the King of Upper and Lower Egypt, Kheper-ka-ra, True of Voice'

---

aHa.n, xw bAq, wDA r Htp, st.f, m r-pr, pn

then Khu-bak, went to rest, seat/throne/place/office.his, in uttereance-house, this

'Then Khu-bak went to rest in his place in this temple'

idnw, n imy-r xtm, ini-sA-Hrt, Smsw.f, aHa.n, dwA-nTr.n.f, n.i, aA r xt nbt

deputy, of overseer seal, Ini-sa-heret, following.him, then, praised-god.of.him, to.me, greatly more-than thing any

'the deputy of the Overseer of the Seal, Ini-sa-Heret, following after him, then thanked god for me greatly more than anything'

---

r Dd, wAD-wy, ir nA, n nTr.f, aha.n rdi.n.f, n.i, aHa n wdnw 10, m bnr-wt, m gs m bHs

to say, fortunate/happy-dual, do these, for god.his, then gave.of.he, for.me, heap/portion of offerings 10, with date-cakes, with half of calf

'to say, 'How fortunate who did these for his god,' then he gave me, ten portions of offerings with date cakes, with half of a calf'

---

aHa.n, sri n kAp, wDA m xd, aHa.n, mAw nA, n kAt

then, official of chamber, went as downstream, then looked at these, of work

'Then the official of the chamber went down stream and inspected the work'

aHa.n.tw, Haiw, im wr, r xt nbt
then.one, rejoiced, therein great, more-than thing any
'Then it was rejoiced greatly, more than anything'

The Stela of Overseer of the House Senwosret

Louvre Museum 272

Htp-di-nswt, wsir xnty imntyw, nb AbDw, rdi.f, pr-xrw t Hnqt, kAw Apdw Ssr mnxt, xt nb nfrt, wab
offering-gives-king, Osiris foremost westeners, lord Abydos, gives.he, invocation-offerings read beer, cattle fowl alabaster cloth, things all good, pure
'An offering which the king gives, Osiris Foremost of the Westeners, Lord of Abydos, he gives invocation offerings of bread, beer, cattle, fowl, alabaster, cloth and all good things pure'

nTr-anxt, im, n kA n, imAxy, imy-r pr, sn-wAsrt, ir.n, Htpt mAat-xrw
god-lives therein, for ka of, honoured, overseer house, Sen-wasret, made.of, Hetepet true-voice
'which the god lives, for the ka of the honoured Overseer of the House, Sen-wasret, born of Hetepet, True of Voice'

Sen-wasret: 'brother/man of Wasret (goddess)'

Wosret: 'The powerful' was a guardian goddess from Thebes (Egyptian: Waset, City of Power) in Upper Egypt. Possibly she was the earliest consort of Amun at Karnak, preceding Mut. Certainly Middle Kingdom pharaohs of Theban origins take her name as an element in their own, such as Sen-Wosret, meaning 'man belonging to Wosret.'

[hieroglyphs]
it in-ti.f-iqr-nb-iri-r-Aw, ir.n xnti-Xti-sAt, mAat-xrw
father.his, Intef-iker-neb-ir-r-aw, made.of Khenti-kheti-sat, true-voice
'His father, Intef-iker-neb-ir-r-aw, born of Sat-khentu-kheti, True of Voice'

Intef-iker-neb-iri-r-aw: 'He who brings his father, excellent lord doer of them all'
Sat-khentu-kheti: 'Daughter of Khenti-kheti' (goddess).

In Egyptian mythology, Khenti-kheti, was a crocodile-god, though he was later represented as a falcon-god. His name means 'foremost retreater.'

[hieroglyphs]
mwt.f, Htpt, ir.n, ipi, mAaat-xrw, nbt-imAx
mother.his, Hetepet, born.of, Ipi, true-voice, possessor-honour
'His mother, Hetepet, born of Ipi, True of Voice, possessor of honour'

snt.f, imny, ir.n, htpt, mAat-xrw   snt.f, Hwt-Hrw-sAt, ir.n, Htpt, mAat-xrw
sister.his, Imeny, born.of, Hetepet, true-voice sister.his, Hat-hor-daughter, born.of, Hetepet, true-voice
'His sister, Imeny, born of Hetepet, True of Voice' **'His sister, Sat-hat-hor, born of Hetepet, True of Voice'**

Sat-hat-hor: 'daughter of Hathor (goddess)'

snt.f, snt-aAmt, irt.n, Htpt, mA-xrw   sn.f, int.f, ir.n, Htpt, mA-xrw, nbt imAxy
sister.his, Senet-aamet, born.of, Hetepet, true-voice, brother.his, Intef, born.of, Hetepet, true-voice, possessor honour
'His sister, Senet-aamet, born of Hetepet, True of Voice, **His brother, Intef, born of Hetepet, True of Voice, possessor of honour'**

Senet-Aamet: 'likeness-Asiatic-woman'

Hmt.f, sAt ipi, ir.n, Hpyw, nbt Aw
wife.his, Sat-Ipi, born.of, Hapyw, possessor of honour
'His wife, Sat-Ipi, born of Hapyw, possessor of honour'

Sat-Ipi: 'Daughter of Ipi (Ipet, Opet)'; Opet (Apet, Ipet, Ipy) was a benign hippopotamus goddess known as a protective and nourishing deity. Her name seems to mean 'harem' or 'favored place'. Our first reference to her comes from the Pyramid Texts, where the king asks that he may nurse at her breast so that he would 'neither thirst nor hunger...forever'. Afterwards, she is called 'mistress of magical protection' in funerary papyri. Under the epithet 'the great Opet',

she is fused to some extent with Ta-weret ![hieroglyph], 'the great one'. Taweret is the protective ancient Egyptian goddess of childbirth and fertility.

Stela of the High Steward Iauti

Louvre Museum 211

A typical heading of funerary stelae: The shen-ring with two seeing Wadjet eyes of Horus, offering eternal protection for the deceased.

nsw di Htp, wsir nb Ddw, nTr aA, Hr ib AbDw

royal give offering, Osiris lord Ddw (Busiris), great-god, upon heart, Abdjw (abydos)

'A royal offering of Osiris, lord of Busiris, great god, living (in the heart of) Abydos'

di.f, prt xrw, kAw Apdw, xt nbt, nfr qbbt

give.he, house-voice (invocation-offerings) bread (**t**)-beer (**hnqt**),
cattle fowl, thing all, beautiful pure

'He gives invocation offerings of bread and beer, cattle and fowl and every good thing pure'

anxt nTr im, ddt pt, qmA(t) tA, innt Hapi3, m Htpw.f

live god therin, give heaven, produce/create land, brings.Happi, in peace.his

'on which a god lives, that the sky gives, the earth creates, and Hapy brings by his grace'

swri mw, Hr bbt

drink water, upon eddy

'drinking water from an eddy,'

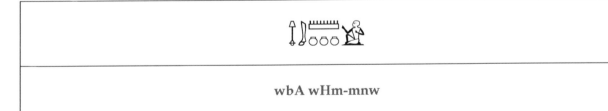

n kA, n imy-pr, sr iAwti, in Hmt.f, s-anx rn.f, Tw-iw-Twiw, wHm anx

for ka, of high-steward (overseer of the house), nobleman Iauti, by wife.his, make-live, name.his, Tjuiw-Tjuiw, repeating life

'For the ka of the High Steward, the nobleman, Iauti, his wife, Tjuiw-Tjuiw, repeating of life, makes his name to live.'

Figure on the right making an offering to Iauti

wbA wHm-mnw

butler (man-servant) Wehem-menu

'The butler Wehem-menu'

A stela containing the Throne Name of Amenemhat III

The top register:

The central titles:

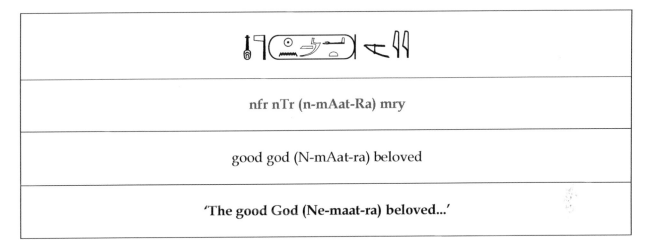
nfr nTr (n-mAat-Ra) mry
good god (N-mAat-ra) beloved
'The good God (Ne-maat-ra) beloved...'

Either side of the central cartouche stands the jackal god standard, Wepwawet and Osiris a **was sceptre** (power) and **anx** (life). Their names are identified as:

wp-wawt
opener-ways
'Wepwawet - the jackal god 'Opener of the Ways'

Wepwawet's titles:

(hieroglyphs)
mry nb-Dsr-xAst
beloved lord sacred (holy)-land
'beloved Lord of the Necropolis'

The Sacred Land being the burial grounds of the West Bank tomb burials.

(hieroglyphs)
wsir
Osiris
'Osiris, god of the Underworld/Afterlife'

(hieroglyphs)
mry wsir xnty-imnt, nTr aA nb
beloved Osiris, foremost-west, god great Abydos
'beloved of Osiris, foremost of the Westerners, great god of Abydos'

Note: the phrase ⬭ **ir.n** or ⬭ **irt.n** 'made.of' translates as 'begotten.of'

---

i, anxw tpiw-tA, wab nb, Xri-HAb nb, sS nb, Hm-kA nb, swAt.sn, Hr abA pn, n Dt

oh, living who-are-on-the-earth, wab priests all, lector priests all, scribes all, ka-priests all, pass.they, upon offering-stone, of eternity

'Oh you living who are upon the earth, all wab-priests, all lector preists, all scribes, all ka-priests, who shall pass by this offering stone of eternity.'

---

mrr.Tn, anx n.Tn, swt.Tn, Hs.Tn, nTrw.Tn, swDA.Tn, iAwt.Tn, Xrdw.Tn, Smsw, Dd.Tn

desire.you, live for.you, king.your, praise.you, gods.your, office/function.your, children.your, eldest, say.you

'(If) you desire that your king would live for you, and your gods would praise you, and (pass on) your duty to your eldest children, you should say:'

Htp-di-nsw, wsir AbDw, di.f, prt-xrw t Hnqt, kAw apdw, Ss-mnxt, snTr mrHt, xt nbt, nfrt wabt

offering-give-king, Osiris Abydos, gives.he, invocation-offerings bread beer, cattle fowl, alabaster clothing, incense ointment, things all, good pure

'A royal offering of Osiris, Lord of Abydos, he gives an invocation offering of bread and beer, cattle and fowl, alabaster and clothing, incense and ointment and every good and pure thing'

---

ddt pt qmA tA, innt Hapy, anx nTr, im

give sky, create earth, brings inundation, live god, therein

'that the sky gives and the earth creates, the inundation brings, on which a god lives.'

---

n kA, n Hmti-n-kf, ir.n, pn-iwyt, n kA, n ifrt, irt.n, imny

for ka, of Hemety-en-kef, made.of, Pen-iuyt, for ka, of Iferet, begotten.of, Imeny

'for the ka of Hemeti-en-kef, begotten of Pen-iuyt, for the kas of Iferet, begotten of Imeny'

Note: the last few lines of the register are incomplete due to damage, but read as follows:

[hieroglyphs]
n kA n, ipiw, ir.n, ifrt   n kA n, mr-s-tx, irt.n, ifrt...
for kA of, Ipiu, begotten of, Ifret, for kA of, Meresetekh, begotten of, Ifret...
'for the ka of Ipiu begotten of Ifret, for the ka of Meresetekh begotten of Ifret...'

[hieroglyphs]
n kA n, att, irt.n, ifrt   n kA n, nw   n kA n, snnw, ir.n...
for ka of, Atet, begotten.of, Ifret for ka of, Nu for ka of, Senenu, begotten of...
'for the ka of Atet begotten of Ifret, for the ka of Nu, for the ka of Senenu...'

[hieroglyphs]
n kA n, r...
for ka of, r...
'for the ka of R...'

Louvre Stela 275

Htp-di-nswt, wsir xnty-imtyw, nTr-aA, nb AbDw, di.f, mw prt-xrw, t Hnqt, kAw Apdw, n imAx, sDAwt Xr-a, aAty mAa-xrw, ms.n Htp, mAat-xrw

offering-king-gives, Osiris foremost westerners, god-great, lord Abydos, gives.he, water invocation-offerings, bread beer, cattle fowl, for honoured-one, seal-bearer under-hand, Aaty, true-voice, born.of Hetep, true-voice

'An offering which the king gives, Osiris Foremost of the Westerners, the Great God, Lord of Abydos, he gives water and invocation offerings of bread, beer, cattle, fowl, for the Honoured One, the Seal Bearer in Charge, Aaty, True of Voice, born of Hetep, True of Voice'

‡ 𓉐 𓏤 𓃣 𓈖 𓏤 𓈖𓈖𓈖 𓊖 𓏏 𓂧 𓈖𓈖𓈖 𓊪 𓏏𓏤 𓎛 𓅓 𓏤 𓂋

Htp-di-nswt, inpw, tp Dw.f, di.f, mw, Hnqt, pr-xrw, t Hnqt Sbw, imAx sDAwt Xr-a

offering-gives-king, Anubis, on mountain.his, gives.he, water, beer, invocation-offerings, bread beer food-offerings, honoured-one seal-bearer, under-hand

'An offering the king gives Anubis on his mountain, he gives water and beer and invocation offerings of bread, beer and food offerings for the honoured one, Seal Bearer in charge'

Anubis: is the Greek name of a wolf-headed god **Inpu** associated with mummification and the afterlife in ancient Egyptian religion. The sacred animal of Anubis has been associated with the jackal. Some wild dogs which roam the Egyptian deserts have similar features to the jackal of long legs, pointed nose, upright ears and lengthy tail.

𓊵 𓅭 𓏤 𓂝 𓈖𓈖𓈖 𓏤 𓄤 𓏏 𓋹 𓏤 𓆛 𓂋 𓏏 𓏏

Htp-wy, mAa-xrw, rn.f, nfr, xut-Xnty, ms.n, inst, mAa-xrw

Hetepuy, true-voice, name,his, good, Khut-khenty, born.of, Inset, true-voice

'Hetepuy, True of Voice, his good name is Khut-khenty, born of Inset, True of Voice'

𓂻𓈖𓏏𓄿... (hieroglyphs)

sn tA, n xnty-imntyw, m prt-aAt, mAA nfrw, nw, wp-wAwt m prt-tpt

kissing land, for Khentyu-Imentyu, in ritual-procession-great, seeing beauty, of Wep-wawt in ritual-procession-first

'Kissing the ground for Khenty-Imentyw in the Great Ritual Procession (of Osiris) and seeing the beauty of Wep-wawt in the First Ritual Procession'

𓀜... (hieroglyphs)

in imAx, sDAwt Xr-a, mry mAa-xrw

by honoured-one, seal-bearer under-hand, Mery true-voice

'by the honoured one, the Seal Bearer in charge*, Mery, True of Voice'

*In charge of the seal

The Stela of the Royal Scribe Maaty

Louvre Museum C89

[hieroglyphs]
Htp-di-nsw, xA (1000), m t Hnqt, kAw Apdw, xt nb, nfrt wabt, n kA.k, nb HH, di.f
offering-gives-king, 1000, bread beer, cattle foul, things every, good pure, for kA.your, lord eternity, gives.he
'An offering which the king gives, of 1000 loaves of bread and beer, cattle and fowl and all good and pure things for the ka of the Lord of Eternity, he gives (says)'

[hieroglyphs]
snb wDA anx, wAH-ib, m sxm, n anx, n kA, n sS-nsw, Xri-Hb, Hr-tp, imy-r iwni, Sps
health prosperity life, kindly/benevolent, in power, of life, for ka, of scribe-king's, under-ritual-book (lector-priest), on-top (chief), overseer-house, Hermonthis, nobleman
'Health, Prosperity, Life, benevolent in power of life, for the ka of the king's scribe, Chief Lector Priest, Overseer of the House of Hermonthis, Nobleman'

[hieroglyphs] , *[hieroglyph]* **iwni** 'Hermonthis'

The modern town of Armant (ancient Egyptian Iuni, known in Greek as Hermonthis), is located about 12 miles south of Thebes, in Egypt. It was an important Middle Kingdom town, which was enlarged during the Eighteenth Dynasty. It is located today in the Luxor Governorate, on the west bank of the Nile. The modern name of the city derives from Iunu-Montu, 'Pillar Town of the war god Montu.'

wsir xnty-imnt, nb AbDw, wnn-nfr, nb tA Dsr, ist wrt, mwt-nTr, nt pt

Osiris foremost-westerners, lord Abydos, Wenen-nefer, lord land sacred,
Isis great, mother-god, lady heaven

'Osiris Foremost of the Westerners, lord of Abydos, Wenen-nefer, lord of the Sacred Land,
Isis the great, mother of the god, Lady of Heaven'

sn-nTr, t Hqt, n kA.k, wsir-mAaty, mAa-xrw

incense, bread beer, for kA.your, Osiris-Maaty, true-voice

'Incense, bread and beer for your ka, Osiris-Maaty, True of Voice'

t Hnqt snw, mw-wDHw, n kA.k, wsir Hry-xrw, mAay, nb imAx

bread beer food-offerings, water-offerings, for ka.your,
Osiris master-voice, Maaty, possessor honour

'Bread, beer and food and water offerings for your ka,
Osiris, Master of Voice, Maaty, possessor of honour'

in sA.f, s-anx, rn.f, nxt-m-wAst, mAa-xrw

by son.his, make-live, name.his, Nekhet-em-Waset, true-voice

'It is his son who makes his name to live, Nekhet-em-Waset, True of Voice'

Hry-xrw Snsy, nbt tAwy, Hsy aA, n wsir, xnty-imntt, mAaty, mAa-xrw, nb imAx

high-voice worship, lady two-lands, favoured great,
of Osiris, foremost-westerners, Maaty, true-voice, possessor-honour

'Heavenly voice of worship, Lady of the Two Lands, greatly favoured of Osiris, Foremost of the Westerners. Maaty, True of Voice, possessor of honour'

---

ink Sd nxn, qrs iAwy, mAry nb, iw rdi.n, t n Hqr, Hsw n HAty

I educate young, bury old, wretched all, I gave.of, bread for hungry, clothes for naked

**'I educated the young and buried all the old and wretched,
I gave bread to the hungry and clothes to the naked'**

The Stela of the Official Mentuhotep

UC 14333 in London

Htp-di-nswt, wsir n Ddw nTr aA, nb AbDw, di.f,
prt-xrw t Hnqt, kAw Apdw, 1000 m Ssrw mnxt

offering-gives-king, Osiris of Busiris, god great, lord Abydos, gives.he,
invocation-offerings bread beer, cattle fowl, 1000 as linen clothing

'An offering which the king gives Osiris of Busiris, the Great God, Lord of Abydos, he gives
invocation offerings of bread, beer and cattle, and 1000 as linen and clothing'

xt nb, nfr wab, n imAx, r-pat HAty-a, imy-r, Hmw-nTr, mTw-Htp, ir.n, Hpy, mAa-xrw

things all, pure good, for honoured, prince nomarch, overseer, servant-god (priests),
Mentju-hetep, begotten.of, Hapy, true-voice

'and all things, pure and good, for the honoured Prince and Nomarch, Overseer of the Priests,
Mentju-hetep, begotten of Hapy, True-of Voice'

Dd.f, ink mn, rwd mDd-wAt, rdi.n, nb.f, mrwt.f, ink aA, n st-StAt, wAH-ib

say.he, I estalished, foot stick-to-the path, give.of, lord.his, love.his, great of place-secrets, kind/patient-heart

'He said, I was enduring whose foot stuck to the path, his lord loved him, great of the place of secrets, kind in heart'

Sw m nhrhr, nn kAhs, xft wAsr

free from hostility, not harsh/overbearing, when powerful-man

'free from hostility, not harsh when a powerful man'

mrwt m Xt, nt smrw, wrw aH, xaw, im, aq, Hr nb.f, wrw Xr pH.f

love therein body, of friends/courtiers, great-ones palace, appearance, therein, enter, upon lord.his, great-ones under end.his

'Love therein the body of courtiers, the great ones of the palace, appearing therein, entering upon the lord and great ones around him'

iriw-sbxt, xAmy, r pH bw, nty, Hm im

door-keepers portal, bow-down, to end place, who/which, majesty therein

'The door-keepers of the portal bowed down until (I) reached where the majesty was'

prr im, ib wAS Hswt, m Hr, n bw-nb

come-out therein, heart be-honoured favoured, in face, of everyone

'Came out of therein, heart honoured and favoured in the face of everyone'

ir.n, Hm.f, nn n bAk.f, n-aAt-n, mDd-wAt, ir.n.f wi, m mH-ib, Hm.f, m iwn, tp spAt.f

did.of, majesty.his, this for servant.his, through-greatness-of, press-on-way (loyal/obedient), did.of.him I, as trusted/confidant majesty.his, in pillar-town (Heliopolis), principal/first nome.his

'His majesty did this for his servant through the greatness of loyalty, he made me his trusted confidant in Iunw (Heliopolis) his principal nome'

rx xm, n Hr mrwt, bw-nb, Hr dwA nTr, Hr nHt, n wAH, tp tA

know ignorant, of upon loved, everyone, upon worship god, upon prayer, live-long, upon earth

**'The wise and ignorant loved (me), everyone thanked god,
praying for (me) to endure upon earth'**

---

n-aA-n, Hss wi, Hm.f, r kwi, xprw, n niwt tn

through-greatness-of, favoured I, majesty.his, more-than me, forms, of town this

'Through greatness his majesty favoured me more than any other being in this town'

---

ink Sd nxn, qrs iAwy mAry nb, wi rdi.n, t n Hqr, Hbsw n HAwty

I educated young, buried old wretched all, I gave.of, bread to hungry, clother to naked

**'I educated the young and buried the old and wretched,
I gave bread to the hungry and clothes to the naked'**

ink sA, npry, hi n tAyt, xpr.n, n.f, sxAt-Hrw, iHw

I son, Nepry, husband of Tayet, become.of, for.it, Sekhat-Heru, cattle

**'I son of Nepry (Grain God), husand of Tayet,
made exist the cattle of Sekhat-Heru (Milk Goddess)'**

---

nb Spssw, m aAtt nb, msxnt, xnmw, ir rmT

possessor riches, as greatly all, abode-of-the-gods, Khnum, made people

'A possessor of all great riches of the abode of the god Khnum, creator of mankind'

---

iw, xpr, n Hapy Sri, rnpt 25, nn rdi Hqr, spat, di.n, n.s Sma-it bdt

behold/is/are, happen, of flood little, year 25, not cause be-hungry, nome,
gave.of, to.it, southern-barley emmer-wheat

**'Behold, a low flood happened in Year 25, I did not cause the district to be hungry, but gave it
southern barley and emmer wheat'**

nn rdi, xpr wgg, im.s, r iwt, Hapyw aAw, snm n Xrd, m dd (rdi-wy) wrH, n xArwt

not cause, happen misery, therein.it, to/until come, flood great, supply-necessities for children, from given-ample-provisions (give-dual), anoint, of widows

'I did not cause misery therein until a high flood came, I supplied necessities for the children from my given ample provisions and anointed the widows'

---

nn nDs, m(A)r, m hAy, aHa.n, r rdit, mrwt n mrwt, nfr rn, mAat-xrw, m Xrt-nTr

not poor-man, wretched, in my-time, fought.of.(i), to cause, love for love, good name, true-voice, in necropolis

'Not a commoner was miserable in my time, I fought to cause to be loved for love, my good name, True of Voice in the Necropolis'

---

sbAwt n Xrdw, m Dd, hrt wAH-ib, tm aHA, Hna nDs, nn Hry kAhs mry

teaching of children, in speaking, peace benevolent-heart, not fight, together-with commoner, not master overbearing beloved

'Teaching children in speaking peace and benevolence and no strife with the commoner, a master who is overbearing is not loved'

hnn ib, r Ddt.f, mArw.f, r skt.f, xrt nt Xt.f, sDm mdw.f, dr mAr.f, rdi s, r wn.f, mAa

attend/consider heart, to says.his, misery.his, to wipe-away/empty.he, state/condition of belly.his, listen words.his, remove-evil misery.his, place man, according-to being.his, true

'Attend the heart to him who speaks his miseries, he who empties the state of his belly, a man is placed according to his true being'

m HAw, gr hrp.tw, ib, xAm rmn, n bw-nb, tm Hbs-Hr r Hqr

in excess of/in-addition-to, silent suppress-one's-desires, heart, bow-down arm, for everyone, not cover-face hungry

'In addition to, (I was) silent, to suppress one's desires of the heart, (I have) bowed down for everyone and not covered the face from the hungry'

drt pw, imAt mrrt, in-m pw, rmT

hand this, charm/gracious desired/loved, disposition, this-it-is people

'A gracious hand is desired, this is the disposition of the people'

nn aHA nb, r rwdw, r xtmw nb, n pr, wpw-Hr, Dd hnn, ib.k

not fight all, against agent, against seal-bearers all, of house,
except/but, say attend-to/consider, heart.your

**'to not fight against all agents, against all seal bearers of the House (Palace),
but say, 'Consider your heart''**

m iwhAw, r sprty, r Dd.f, iit.n.f, Hr.s, smi mDAt, n irt, nDs ,XArwt, nmH r xtmt

not load/burden, against petitioner, until says.he, came.of.he, upon.it, report/complaint papyrus-
scroll, to do, commoner, widow, orphan, to contract

**'Do not burden against the petitioner, until he comes and speaks, when the complaint papyrus
book to make a contract with the commoner, the widow and orphan'**

ir nt.s, n rw, r snf, nty wA r mAr

make of.it, of fraction (3 quarters), to make breathe/succour, who/which one misery

'To make breathe a fraction of one who is in misery'

wn biAt, nfrt nt s, n.f, r dd (rdi.wy) xAw, m-irrt

indeed character/qualities/marvels, good of man, to.him, more-than doubly-giving 1000, in-fact

**'Indeed, in fact, the good character of a man is worth more to him
than giving a thousand times'**

iw sDm-r, n rmT, m tAs pf, Hry r nDsw

behold, testimony, of people, as declaration this/that master/chief/senior to small/commoner

**'Behold, this testimony of the common people,
is heard as that speech from the senior to the inferior**

---

mnw pw, n s, nfrw.f, smx pw, bin biA

monument this-it-is, of man, goodness.his, forget this bad character

'The monument of a man, this it is his goodness, the bad character is forgotten'

ir wn xpr, mi Dd, wnn rn.n, nfr, mn m niwt, nn wAsi, mnw n Dt

now/then exist/happens. like say, be name.of, good, enduring in town, not ruined, monument of eternity

'Now if it happens like said my name will be good and enduring in the city, my eternal monument will not be ruined'

The Stela of Tagemirmut

Museum of Fine Arts 51.2149, Budapest

The deceased woman standing on the right has her arms raised in adoration of the Solar Bark deities: Ra-Herakhety, Atum, Khepri, Isis and Nephthys

𓊹 (hieroglyphs)
bHdt nTr aA (Hrw-Axty) bHdt nTr aA
Behdetite, great god (Horus-Akhety) Behdetite, great god
'Horus-Akhety (Horus of the Two Horizons), the Behdetite (Edfu), Great God'

(hieroglyphs)
Htp-di-nsw, ra-Hrw-Axty, nTr aA, nb pt nTrw, itmw, nTr nb tAwy, iwnw, xpri nTr xpr Ds.f
offering-gives-king, Ra-Herakhety, god great, lord heaven gods, Atum, god lord two-lands, Heliopolis, khepri god created self.him
'An offering which the king gives Ra-Herakhety, the Great God, Lord of the Sky and gods, Atum, god and lord of the Two Lands and Heliopolis, Khepri the god who created himself'

(hieroglyphs)
rdi.snw, pr-xrw t Hnqt, kAw Apdw, irp irtt, sn-nTr, Ssr mnxt, xt nb nfr, anx nTr, im
give.they, invocation-offerings bread beer, cattle fowl, wine milk, incense, linen clothing, things all good, lives god, therein
'They give invocation offerings of bread, bear, cattle, fowl, wine, milk, incense, linen and clothing and all good things on which the god lives therein'

n kA n, Hwt-hrw-tA-gm-ir-mwt, mAa-xrw, ms Dd-ist-iw-s-anx

for ka of, Hat-hor-Ta-gem-ir-mut, true-voice, born Djed-Iset-Iu-s-ankh

'for ka of, Hat-hor-Ta-gem-ir-mut, True of Voice, born of Djed-Iset-Iu-s-ankh'

USEFUL VOCABULARY

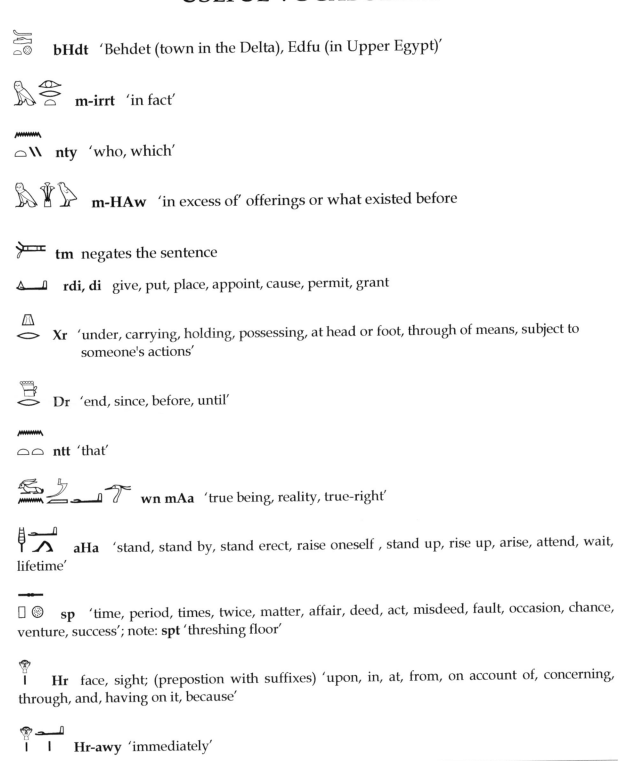

bHdt 'Behdet (town in the Delta), Edfu (in Upper Egypt)'

m-irrt 'in fact'

nty 'who, which'

m-HAw 'in excess of' offerings or what existed before

tm negates the sentence

rdi, di give, put, place, appoint, cause, permit, grant

Xr 'under, carrying, holding, possessing, at head or foot, through of means, subject to someone's actions'

Dr 'end, since, before, until'

ntt 'that'

wn mAa 'true being, reality, true-right'

aHa 'stand, stand by, stand erect, raise oneself , stand up, rise up, arise, attend, wait, lifetime'

sp 'time, period, times, twice, matter, affair, deed, act, misdeed, fault, occasion, chance, venture, success'; note: **spt** 'threshing floor'

Hr face, sight; (prepostion with suffixes) 'upon, in, at, from, on account of, concerning, through, and, having on it, because'

Hr-awy 'immediately'

𓁷𓅓 **Hr-m** 'why?'

𓁷𓋴𓄿 **Hr-sA** 'upon, outside, after, in turn'

𓏏 **ti** phonetic sound **ti,** enclitic particle: **yes, yeah**

𓏏𓏭 **ti** phonetic sound **ti,** enclitic particle: **yes, yeah**

𓊢𓈖 **aHa.n** introduces narrative past tense: 'pay attention to this, listen to this'

𓂦𓌠 **tr** 'forsooth, pray'

𓅂 **A** enclitic particle, with exclamatory force 'A!'

𓈖𓅂 **nA** 'this, these, here, the, hither'

𓇋𓋴𓏏𓊪 **ist** 'lo'

𓂋𓆑 **rf** 'now, then'

𓇋𓂋𓏥 **iry** 'thereof, thereto'

𓇋𓂋 **ir** 'as to, if'

𓇋𓂋𓏭 **iry** 'thereof, thereto'

𓏏𓅱 **tw** 'you, your, one, this, that'

𓇋𓋴 **is** 'after all, indeed, even, in fact'

𓇋𓏤 **iw** 'is, are, behold' starts a sentence

𓁷𓄖 **tp-Hsb** 'reckoning, standard, rectitude (high moral standard)' lit. in front of reckoning

𓊪𓏤 **pw** 'It is, They are, this, who? what? whichever?

𓇋𓐠 **ix** 'then, therefore, what?'

𓐍𓂋 **xr** non enclitic particle: 'and, further'; auxillary verb: 'so says'; preposition: 'with, near, under (a king), speak (to), by (of agent)'

𓂋𓎡 **rk** 'but, now'

𓐍𓆑𓏏 **xft** (preposition) 'in front of, in accordance with, as well as, corresponding to'; when, according to, at the time of, when, (speech) to (someone)

Note: 𓅓 **m** enclitic particle (not translated); 'behold'; preposition 'in the hand, possession, charge of, together with, from'; imperative 'take'; interogative 'who, what'

𓉔𓋹𓅱𓊪𓈖𓌀𓇳𓌀

'May you be given: Life - Prosperity - Health Forever and Ever'

http://arkpublishing.co.uk

Made in the USA
Lexington, KY
23 November 2016